29 Reasons Not To Go To Law School

Revised Edition With Two Bonus Reasons
&
The Ten Best Lawyer Jokes

29 Reasons Not To Go To Law School

Revised Edition With Two Bonus Reasons
&
The Ten Best Lawyer Jokes

Typesetting & Design: Cynara Branden
Aurora Type

■ ■ ■

First Printing: August 1982
Second Printing: January 1983
Revised Edition: May 1984

ISBN 0-917316-87-8
Library of Congress Catalog Card Number: 82-99889

Thank You:

The nicest thing about doing this book, except for the pleasure of working with each other, has been the good energy and support we have received from hundreds of former law students and lawyers. To say the least, most people still have intense feelings about the subject and it would have been easy to retitle our book "**129** Reasons Not To Go To Law School." Particular thanks to all of those whose signed comments appear herein. For several, contributing was an act of courage.

In addition we would like to specially thank Anne Strick, whose fine book *Injustice For All* is the source of much of the material in Reason 10, Bob Keller, whose article "All the News That's Fit to Chuckle Over—Newspaper Humor in the Old West," published in the *Annals of Wyoming*, provided the quotes that appear from the *Cheyenne Leader*, and Michael Lowy and Craig Haney, whose article "The Creation of Legal Dependency: Law School in a Nutshell" in *The People's Law Review* was the inspiration for Reason 12. The Will of a Roman Citizen in Reason 16 is from *Western Civilization, An Urban Perspective*, Volume 1, by F. Roy Willis.

A number of people made suggestions that were invaluable. Thanks to Jean Allen, **Dan Armistead**, Denis Clifford, Hayden Curry, Janice Kosel, Selma Mann, Carol Pladsen, Eddie Warner and Andromache Warner.

Preparing for Exams

Table of Contents

Introduction

CAUTION: The message you will read here is subversive of a cherished American folk fantasy—the one in which the sons and daughters of Pullman porters, shoe store clerks and cowboys go to the University, get awarded a Juris Doctorate degree and live happily ever after in the suburbs. Or, to be more lyrical, "Mama, Don't Let Your Babies Grow Up To Be Lawyers!"*

Our thesis is simple—lawyering in the U.S., which has traditionally been one of the major crossroads where power and status merge to produce six figure incomes, simply isn't what it used to be. Indeed, these days so many power-hungry young barristers are competing to pay the rent on their Porsches that getting a law license almost guarantees one gridlock in a traffic jam of stalled careers.

And if one trouble with being a lawyer is that it just isn't the field it used to be, the main difficulty with law school is that it's exactly the institution it always was—still featuring the teaching methods of the Spanish Inquisition combined with a curriculum so enamored

---

*Our apologies to Willie Nelson.

with the nineteenth century that it barely notices the twentieth and absolutely won't concede that a new one lurks just around the next decade.

With this introduction you have surely guessed that our goal is to stick pins into the plump balloons of legal training and practice. As so much of the legal establishment is kept aloft on hot air, our task is embarrassingly easy. So simple, in fact, that we happily plead guilty to excessive enthusiasm. You might even feel that we are a bit one-sided. But then, remember, we were trained as lawyers and our first lesson was "It never pays to be fair."

LAW SCHOOL

Reasons 1 – 4:
Fellow Students

1. The Drudge

Most law students don't want to get romantically involved with other law students. After studying law all day, who wants to talk it all night?

But during third year, a friend began dating a particularly intense classmate.

"How can you spend time with her?" I asked. "All she talks about is contracts, torts and criminal procedure."

"That's the idea," he said. "It's great bar review."

Ron Ostroff
George Washington University School of Law
Currently: Writer, *The Kansas City Times*

You can quickly identify this genderless type by the piquant but unmistakeable musty odor it acquires the first week of fall semester when for 102 consecutive hours it literally barricades itself at the end of a library table behind a mountain of casebooks, hornbooks, annotated codes, federal reporters, legal encyclopedias, law dictionaries and law reviews. While seeing the drudge at work may initially make you smile, your good humour will last only until you realize that there are dozens of drudges in your class that all live behind veritable Matterhorns, Everests and Kilamanjaros of legal material. The cumulative effect of all this anal drudge-hoarding is that you will never ever find any assigned book on its proper shelf and will inevitably spend long hours futilely exploring the hills and valleys of drudgedom. For reasons that may have almost as much to do with its aversion to light and air as to its fear that a potentially needed bit of information will escape, no true drudge ever reshelves a book.

The drudge's most inspiring characteristic is its iron constitution, exhibited by:

1. Its ability to go for days without sleep and three years without sex.
2. Its ability to thrive without any exposure to natural light. Once a drudge enters the physical plant of the law school, it lives much like the gollum in its subterranean cavern, emerging pasty-faced and blinking on the day of the Bar Exam.
3. The ox-like endurance required to carry pockets filled to the brim with the change needed to feed its closest companions—

The Drudge

At Work

At Leisure

On a Date

the law school machines. In particular, the drudge has an intimate relationship with the photo copier as it stands for hours faithfully reproducing every bit of recommended reading, every case cited in every footnote, every obscure minority opinion and every word written by every professor in the law school, oblivious to the line of other students waiting to copy a page or two.
WARNING! While drudges are normally mild, lethargic and slow to anger, they can turn momentarily vicious if you come between them and their favorite Xerox machine.

4. The ability to exist exclusively on the processed cardboard and tepid liquids available from the vending machines in the student lounge (reason enough for most people not to go to law school). Indeed, the drudge appears to ingest with relish:

   ★ a coffee-like beverage that comes out of the same plastic tube as a liquid the vending company humorously refers to as chicken soup;
   ★ beef and bean burritos that manage to stay cold in the center no matter how long they are left in the microwave;
   ★ ice-cream drumsticks with leaky bottoms that taste like the glue used on the bindings of West's Federal Reporters.

2. The Compulsive Talker

The first day of school I was abashed by the confident few who spouted legal lingo like erudite magpies. It took me a few weeks to see that they weren't generally the brighter students. Then I realized a sad thing—the vastly more sophisticated professors were only pretending to take these talkative students seriously. In fact they were setting them up, maneuvering them closer and closer to the abyss of midterm exams. When most of them crashed, they were never heard from again.

Jerry Carlin
Yale Law School
Currently: Painter

This is the fellow student you will find hardest to take. Although the compulsive talker looks pretty much like other students, he or she is not hard to recognize because:

1. Their right hand is usually seen waving frantically overhead in class and by the second year is locked permanently in an overhead position.
2. Their voice is almost always loud, strident and shrill.
3. Although content of their classroom remarks vacillate between the painfully obvious, the painfully dumb and the painfully obnoxious, compulsive talkers are almost always transparently pleased with themselves.
4. They shout out answers to rhetorical questions (unsolicited and usually wrong).
5. They hide behind posts near lecture room doors before and after class (and in the stairwell by the library on weekends) from where they swoop down like a crow from a clothesline to alternately interrogate and berate fellow students. They specialize in bizarre questions on unread footnotes and endless diatribes extolling the brilliance and crucial importance of a dissenting opinion that their unsuspecting quarry hadn't known existed. Indeed, the compulsive talker is usually hoping that you haven't read the piece of esoterica in question so that he can first feel superior and then fill you in ad nauseum. Your best way of dealing with this attack is not to respond. Chances are, the C.T. will be so busy carrying on a lively and even contentious dialogue with himself that he will soon forget you are there.

The Compulsive Talker

At Work

At Leisure

6. They do poorly on exams, to the surprise of no one but themselves.
7. They pass the Bar Exam on the second try and take jobs as assistant district attorneys in charge of prosecuting traffic tickets.

YOU'RE GOING TO LOVE THIS...
AND DON'T WORRY I'LL EXPLAIN
ALL THE IN-BITS... YOU KNOW..
FROM MY OWN PERSONAL
EXPERIENCE AND ALSO...

On a Date

NOTHING TO DECLARE

3. The Book Stealer

As each quarter drew to a close, fear of one's classmates gaining an unfair advantage mounted ominously. No one was exempt from suspicion. "See that blind man?" someone in the library would whisper. "I'll bet he is a first year student with 20/20 vision. He's probably escaping with the new Supreme Court abortion decision rolled into the hollow tip of his cane."

Kathy Reigstad
University of Washington School of Law
Currently: Production Editor, Harper & Row

Equipment Needed: One razor blade (preferably single-edged).

M.O.:* Finds dark corner of library stacks. Uses razor blade to quickly slice out newly assigned pages of casebooks, legal encyclopedias, etc. Hides them inside underclothing. Students who go without have been known to use their body cavities, although this method obviously cuts down on volume, so even the most liberated book stealer eventually gets either jockey shorts or a bra with a 38 cup.

Purpose: Occasionally to gain uninterrupted possession of "particularly important" reserve material. More commonly to deny other students access to the information.

Identifying Characteristics: Always goes straight home after using library. Signs up for job interviews with all government security agencies.

---

*We describe here only the modus operandi of the most common sub-species of the book stealer genus—the budget book stealer. Other sub-species include the plutocrat book stealer, who checks out all important reserve books a week before exams, locks them in his/her locker and pays fines with treasury notes; the radical book stealer, who defaces important books with the sayings of Chairman Mao in red nail polish, et cetera.

The Book Stealer

4. The Paranoid

*First year before exams the fear was so heavy that you could
see it, taste it, even walk on it. When the first exam began
I was the only one who was mellow. Of course, I always
hold my right wrist with my left hand to keep it from
shaking.*

Ted Massey
University of Minnesota Law School
Currently: Advocate for Low Income Persons

As a class, paranoids are ever-vigilant, their reflexes honed to a razor's
edge. For example, one famous Harvard law paranoid would, at the
merest interrogative look from a professor, jump out of his seat, and
do two somersaults while reciting seven alternative holdings for the
case under discussion, concluding with "Not prepared, sir," all before
the professor even had a chance to check the seating chart to call on
the person two rows behind.

At Work

At Leisure

SAY ISN'T THAT YOUR TORTS PROFESSOR OVER THERE?

On a Date

Unfortunately true, paranoids can be hard to spot. In an atmosphere where suspicion will almost always get you further than generous understanding and where it rarely pays to dabble in truth and justice when you can more quickly score points by finding an Achille's heel or picking nits, all but a few law students would seem to qualify. One law professor of our acquaintance has, however, developed what she considers to be a sure way to separate garden-variety law students from true paranoids. She calls it her "easy test ploy," and it involves no more than giving an exam consisting of only simple and obvious questions. True paranoids always flunk. Able to accept nothing at face value, they always assume that the straightforward only exists to mask the circuitous and therefore fill their blue books with every answer save the right one. By contrast, the average—mildly paranoid—student manages to pass, albeit with a poor grade—hanging on to a slender thread of common sense which allows him/her to allude to the obvious answer before diluting and embroidering it with a myriad of alternative solutions. Those who do well on this exam tend not to make it through the first year.

Because believing in everything and nothing simultaneously requires such studious, although schizophrenic attention, some paranoids eventually throw in their delusions and metamorphose into Drudges (see Reason 1). You can usually identify these hybrid creatures through their relationship to the coffee machine. They approach with drudge-like determination, produce a quarter from bulging pockets, insert it resolutely and then jump back three paces in case it blows up like the one in *Flackey v. City of Tampa*, 620 U.S. 889.

Reason 5:

Classrooms

*Much of what went on in a law school lecture was like
a bad melodrama. The professors, who awarded themselves
the only starring role, were more interested in winning argu-
ments and hogging center stage than supplying information.*

Tony Mancuso
Hastings College of Law, University of California
Currently: Jazz musician/writer

Atmosphere: Ponderous and permeated with bloodlust. Even the
heartiest student feels like a Christian hors d'oeuvre served up to the
law professor lion. Grooves worn into the edge of the desks by the
fearfully clutching fingers of generations of student victims awaiting
their turn for public humiliation bear further testimony to the quasi-
religious roots of the law.

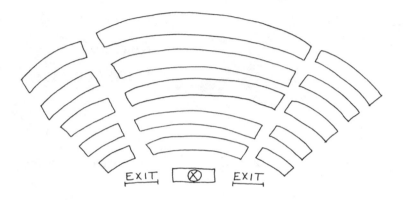

EXIT ⊗ EXIT

Design: Ingeniously modeled along the lines of a Roman gladiatorial arena. Professors equipped with the dread instrument of torture known as the Seating Chart can easily single out and nail their hopeless victims. Why hopeless? First, as the floor plan illustrates, there is nowhere to hide and escape is made awkward by the deliberate placement of the doors at the professor's back, leaving students as exposed as babes on a freeway and almost as vulnerable. Second, and even more subversive to one's mental health, is the jeopardy in which one's psyche is placed. If you should miraculously manage to produce a right answer it will never be sufficient. You will always be questioned

further, lead onward with more and more recondite hypotheticals until you inevitably fail. For this, you see, is the Socratic Method run amok and you play but two roles—fall guy or straight man—depending on whether the professor casts himself as prosecutor/persecutor or as the suave master of subtle nuance and gentle mockery. Either way the result will be the same—the professor will have the last word and you will feel used and foolish.*

A bit of advice: When called on, always respond "Not prepared." While some professors claim to grade on class performance, most are too busy savoring the distress of their next victim to keep track.

---

*Looking on the bright side, first hand experience with the art of humiliation can be viewed as an advantage of going to law school as it will serve you in good stead as you spend your life seeking to humiliate others.

Reason 6:
Casebooks — The Law Student's Burden

Toward the middle of my first year I had a rare moment of enlightenment. Timidly I approached my favorite professor —the only one who didn't inspire fear in my heart. "It's just a thought," I began apologetically, "but is it possible that . . . well, it's crazy and I can't imagine why they would do it . . . but, it seems to me that some of these cases begin to make a little sense if you believe that the judge made up his mind which way he wanted to rule and then twisted the facts and the law to fit. Is that possible?" I asked, horrified at the thought that anyone so exalted could do something so diabolical, so crass, so obvious. The good man laughed and put his arm around my shoulder. "Welcome to the law," he said.

Dianna Waggoner
New College of California School of Law
Currently: Free-lance journalist

Physical Appearance: There are three principal colors—bruise blue, open-wound red and bile green.

Size: Not a one under five pounds—they are weighty in this sense, if in no other.

Guts: Deadly, double-columned rows of small tight type with even duller, smaller rows of footnotes guaranteed to make you squint until you scream. They are unrelieved by graphic design, color, illustration or common sense.

Style: A rhetorical one which can be described as Baroque Legalese; literal corpulence; miles of print searching for an inch of meaning; inane repetition of the obscure; obtuse overkill in extremis (if we went on for another page you would clearly get the idea).

The Intimate Albatross Factor: Professors, who know more about guilt-inducing than the I.R.S. and almost as much as your mother, insist that you have their leaden tome in your possession at all times. It's up to you whether you:

★ clutch them to your bosom;
★ strap them to your back;
★ stuff them into a briefcase, satchel, bikebag or wheelbarrow; or
★ employ two sherpas and a llama.

Message: From grammar school through college your books have always had a point to them, a fairly straightforward lesson to be learned. Math books teach you that $1 + 1 = 2$. Spanish books teach you that uno, dos, tres = one, two, three. Anatomy books teach

35

you more than you want to know about how philogyny divided by ontogyny somehow equals your appendix. Above all, the instruction process within these textbooks is orderly. Juan y Maria learn to say "Buenos Dias" before they tackle windmills with Don Quixote.

When it comes to casebooks, however, the simple can never be counted on to precede the complex. They are as full of the written reports of cases that reach the wrong result for the wrong reason as they are with those that reach the right result for the right reason. And then there are the nonsensical anomalies—decisions that have apparently been included only to demonstrate the absurdity of the judicial retirement system which forces no judge to step down who can still find the way to the bathroom.

If casebooks are so awful, why haven't they been abandoned? Among other reasons:

★ they are the time honored dinosaurs of a profession that only reluctantly substituted school for the apprenticeship method of reading random judicial decisions in the hope that they would eventually make sense;

★ the essential nonsense of the casebook method pleasantly enhances the power of the professor as the fount of all wisdom;

★ law professors, as a rule, don't themselves have to read them, relying instead on "Teachers' Cheat Editions." These not only provide simple summaries of each case but also contain numerous hypothetical questions (with answers) cleverly designed to torment even the most stubborn of students.

HURRY UP- I HAVE TO STUDY!

HURRY UP- SHE HAS TO STUDY!

Reason 7:
Weekends

There are no weekends in law school. The beauty of Saturday and Sunday is only that there are no classes to interrupt studying. But in my 3 years there was the one great exception:

On a warm Friday afternoon I met Karen on Telegraph Avenue. She had long hair, beads, a great smile and no bra. She took me to her apartment—it had a great view— not a law book in sight. We took LSD and I was her student until Monday morning when I found myself back in my Contracts class watching the words wiggle like worms in my casebook and the sun set on the blackboard behind the professor's head.

Michael Zeitsoff
Boalt Hall School of Law, University of California
Currently: Songwriter

WE'LL BE ALONE AT LAST!

The Ski Weekend

Equipment List:
- 1 Torts casebook
- 2 yellow legal pads
- 1 Contracts casebook
- 2 Gilbert's Outlines (Real Property and Criminal Law)
- 3 class notebooks
- 1 bottle No-Doz
- 1 bottle eyedrops
- 3 pens

Helpful Hint: Long woolen underwear is helpful for studying past 2 a.m. and a colorful hat and scarf will get you into the spirit of the weekend. Don't bother with skis, however—you won't have time to use them.

The Super Bowl Weekend

Planning Ahead:
- Sat. 5:00 a.m.—Awake and complete Moot Court brief (approximate time, 10 hours*)
- Sat. 3:00 p.m.—Go to law library, work on contracts research paper (approximate time, 9 hours)
- Sun. 5:00 a.m.—Start reading and briefing cases for Monday's classes —Contracts, Civil Procedure and Remedies (approximate time, 8½ hours)

---

*All time allotments allow for vending machine and toilet usage.

Sun. 2:00 p.m.—Sit down in front of T.V. to enjoy game

Sun. 2:08 p.m.—Fall asleep just after kick-off

Sun. 4:49 p.m.—Wake up as game ends and head for law library

Helpful Hint: You will want to resolve not to waste so much time next weekend.

The Lost Weekend

(with an old lover who turns up and won't take
"Sorry, I'm behind in Crim Law" for an answer)

Equipment List:

1 cassette tape, *The Joy of Guilt*

1 self-help book, *Up from Celibacy: A Guidebook for Lapsed Monks and Others Who Have Forgotten How or Never Knew*

1 reference book, *The Non-Lawyer's Guide to Common Legal Slang* (for your friend)

Helpful Hint: Don't bother with birth control devices—your attempt at total withdrawal from manic study will amost surely be too anxiety producing to allow for their use. Be prepared for your self-control to snap within an hour of arriving at the romantic cabin. It is perfectly normal to pull your real property outline from the folds of your merry widow, your criminal procedure book from under the back seat of the car and the Uniform Commercial Code from the picnic basket. At this point you will probably feel pretty desperate. To regain equilibrium, lock yourself in the equipment closet with your books, shut your eyes and pretend you never left the law library.

WE'LL BE ALONE AT LAST!

Reason 8:
Personal Transformation
(a.k.a. Creeping Lawyer-Think)

I don't agree with the premise of this book one bit. For me, the study of law was extremely important, I might even say crucial to my career. There is just no way that I would have achieved my great success without it.

Anonymous
University of Texas School of Law
Currently: Gentleman sinsemilla farmer,
　　　　Humboldt County, CA

On Seeing an Auto Accident

CAN I HELP?

Before Law School

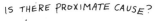

IS THERE PROXIMATE CAUSE?

Mid Law School

HERE'S MY CARD.

After Law School

On Seeing a Former Lover

YOU LOOK GREAT,
LET'S GET TOGETHER
LATER.

Before Law School

OH HI—NO I'M
TOO BUSY FOR
COFFEE.

Mid Law School

I'LL DROP BY JUST AS
SOON AS YOU SIGN THIS
LITTLE PAPER THAT SAYS
WE'RE JUST FRIENDS,
MY INCOME IS MINE,
YOU HAVE NO CLAIM TO...

After Law School

Before Law School | Mid Law School | After Law School

On Seeing a Slippery Spot on a Supermarket Floor

Before Law School

Mid Law School

After Law School

Reason 9:
Backs, Eyes & Mononucleosis

For three years, the stacks of law books I lugged about gave me a chronic backache, as well as eye strain and a generally depressed outlook on the world. When I graduated from law school and became a fisherman, I almost tossed them out. That would have been a terrible mistake. Prosser On Torts, Black's Law Dictionary and all the rest have finally become extremely useful tools. I use them to press smoked salmon into lox.

Richard Bell
Hastings College of Law,
University of California
Currently: Salmon fisherman

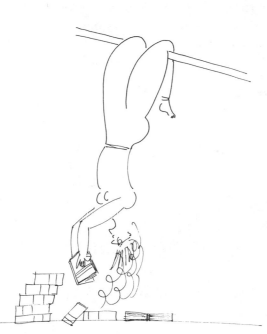

During your three years of pre-Esquire servitude you are almost guaranteed to develop one or all of the following physical deformities: bad eyes, bad back, and mononucleosis.*

Bad Eyes: The cause of this condition is pretty CLEAR (unless you're a law student who hasn't yet seen an optometrist, in which case you will be squinting). Each year law students read the equivalent, both in volume and interest, of six Manhattan phonebooks, three Sears Roebuck catalogues and the collected works of Anthony Trollope. *Caveat:* Incipient blindness is usually accompanied by a fairly noticeable wrinkling of the brow. This can be turned into a considerable asset later on in your career as clients often mistake it for a look of intense professional concern.

Bad Backs: Not as severe as Quasimodo's condition but a definite curvature of the spine occurs after three years of relentless hunching over Prosser on Torts, Williston on Contracts and Louisell on Pleading. Some students try to avoid this condition by studying while hanging upside down from inversion boots. Pink faces and long stringy necks make it easy to identify this group.

Mononucleosis: This disease was invented long ago by law students searching for a rational explanation for terminal boredom. It is

---

*More serious maladies are also common but our editor correctly points out that there is a limited market for lists of lethal diseases.

characterized by exhaustion, nausea and anxiety. When consulted, doctors normally shrug and smile maliciously, having felt even worse in med school. Sufferers—and that includes almost all law students with the exception of the Drudge (see Reason 1)—want to go to bed and pull a cover over their heads for three years. Those who do report a 100% cure rate. The great suffering majority, however, take two aspirin and plug along, saving their bile for that satisfying day when they file their first medical malpractice action.

Reason 10:
Language

I remember one day in Property class. We were on the topic of covenants and had just finished discussing whether they were executed or executory, express or implied, general or specific, principal or auxiliary, joint or several, inherent or collateral or just plain disjunctive, when the professor nailed this poor guy at the back of the class. He cleared his throat and asked, "Mr. Wason, tell us about the springing uses of covenants that run with the land."

That was the last straw for Mr. Wason. He jumped from his seat, spilled his books onto the floor and then, looking like a crazed space cadet, started babbling about "springing, jumping, leaping, bounding, twirling, flying uses . . ." When he finally wound down he just ran out of the classroom.

Phaedra B. Dadra
University of Santa Clara School of Law
Currently: Food Consultant

You there. You with your A+ term papers and secret poems hidden under your shiny new bachelor's degree. You probably think that you are a competent, perhaps even facile speaker of the Queen's English. In fact, it may well be your ability to make words do back flips in mid-sentence that leads you to contemplate a career in a profession which uses them as both spear and shield.

Before you sign up for the LSAT, though, take a closer look at the official language spoken by the Lords and Ladies of the Court of Law. Ah, we're in luck, here comes the great law lord Gobbledygook now. Let's listen for a minute...

You say you can't understand a thing he is saying, but he seems to be saying whatever he is saying at least twice and often thrice and quite impressive it all sounds, too.

Remarkable. You obviously have a quick and intuitive ear. Without a doubt you have the knack to pick up legal language in record time. To help you, let's scrutinize a few of Gobbledygook's favorite phrases:

Pray the Court: Archaic English

Voir Dire: Obsolete French

Oyer, trouver: Archaic English descended from Obsolete French

Perturbatrix (a woman who breaks the law): Whimsical

Certiorari: Middle English from Latin

Mens rea, pendente lite, res adjudicata, assumpsit: Latin

Gebocced: Anglo-Saxon

Garathinx: Old Lombardic

The Great God Gobbledygook and His Devotees

Hereditaments: Sicilian and Neapolitan
Fee simple, equitable title, proximate cause, insanity...: Familiar words
    that have special legal meanings

You say these seem to be no more than bits of jargon and not a language at all.

Right you are again. Legalese is not a language on the order of French or Spanish or even Pig Latin, all of which share a logical structure and internal coherence. With these languages, once the rules are learned, comprehension is close behind. Not so with the language of the law. Each term or phrase is its own arbitrary, mind boggling mystery—vowels and consonants dragged from the scrapheap of history bearing no logical relationship to one another and conveying no meaning that could not be put more easily in English.

But surely, you say, there must be some reason for using all this jargon to obfuscate what seem to be simple enough concepts?

Of course there is, and it goes far beyond the words themselves, straight to the core of the profession: *acquisitive circumlocutio in gross.*

What's that mean?

Why, the longer the words, the higher the fee, of course.

Reason 11:
Low-Level Latrinalia

Someone ran a contest on the wall of a toilet stall in the Women's Restroom as to which law professor you would like to spend a weekend with on a deserted island.
The winner: a vibrator, hands down.

Anonymous
University of Alabama School of Law
Currently: G. O. at Club Med

In graffiti veritas...

i Feel like im all alone.

Kiss Freedom goodbye!

DOCTORS TAKE THE HIPPOCRATIC OATH
LAWYERS TAKE THE OATH OF HYPOCRISY

FINALS ARE HELL ON YOUR SEXLIFE
WHATEVER YOUR SEXUAL ORIENTATION!

What sex life?

Lawyers teach corruption
to the unwary

NUKE HARVARD

Law School - The Opium of Law

Statistics are like lawyers,
they can never be trusted.

YOU FAIL TO CONSIDER THAT
STATISTICS SAY THAT LAWYERS
ARE LIARS SO LAWYERS CAN'T
BE LIARS

OFF THE WALLS OF BOALT HALL SCHOOL OF LAW

52

The law is a bright light
which blinds all Reasonable men

LAWYERS SUCK MONEY $

SHE OFFERED HER HONOR
HE HONORED HER OFFER
AND ALL NIGHT LONG
IT WAS HONOR AND OFFER

After the law fell down
no one was found who could
make it stand

NICE TRY BUT STICK TO
SMOKING HASH

Help! Help.
It's FINALS &
I'M CRACKING UP!

UNIVERSITY OF CALIFORNIA

FUCK THE LAW
BEFORE THE LAW
FUCKS YOU

Amen!

53

Reason 12:
Ego Death, or
Learning to Think Like a Lawyer

*Law school violates not only your basic constitutional right
of freedom of speech, but your even more precious personal
right to think for yourself. Oh, you may try to resist for
a while, but unless you are truly "mad" in the best sense
of that word, law school will eventually mold you into one
of its clones.*

Elaine Kowall
Boalt Hall School of Law, University of California
Currently: Director of CAMBERJ Educational Program

The first day of law school:

A middle-aged professor stands in front of a roomful of bright, confident, articulate students. All have worked hard and gotten top grades for years. They are in a good mood, plainly delighted by what they regard as a new challenge. In contrast the professor seems a bit washed out and haggard. Several students wonder if he is up to the job ahead.

The 10th day:

By now the professor has assigned and discussed a few hundred cases. They are presented out of context and out of order. An 1840 decision from a Massachusetts court follows one decided in Los Angeles in 1957 which in turn comes after a 14th century English opinion. When a particular decision appears to make internal sense, students gratefully grasp at it as they might a life raft on a stormy sea. Unfortunately, their slender hold on security is soon washed away by the next wave of cases which manage on similar facts to arrive at several completely different conclusions. The cases do, however, have one thing in common—they all introduce new jargon and unfamiliar concepts which are nowhere defined. Students, mostly undergraduate social science majors, desperately try to fathom the basic principles on which the new material rests by invoking the tried and true problem solving techniques. The professor airily dismisses these attempts not merely as wrong or unworkable, but with the most damning indictment of all: "They simply are not *legal*."

Interim result:

Confusion and disorientation are rampant and most students conclude that the only way to get through the material is to dig harder and faster. Others become depressed and think of quitting. A few do, breathing great sighs of relief. The majority, who have elected to stay, take two uppers and pretend not to notice.

The 20th day:

The professor has become more demanding. Students who persist in trying to see legal information in the context of a larger worldview are routinely humiliated. Those who look no further than what Justice Marshall said in *Marbury v. Madison* and refer confidently to the rule in Shelley's case are praised. As a result, fewer students persist in invoking considerations of good, bad, right or wrong, more resolve to "think like lawyers."

Interim result:

Long gone are the days when the students seemed bright and brash. Indeed, several have contracted mononucleosis (see Reason 9) and a few have begun to stutter. Several more students drop out but are viewed as failures by the ones who remain.

The 30th day:

The professor is quite relaxed now, almost friendly. Any hope students may have held of relating their law school experience to the larger picture has given way to a feverish determination to master the technicalities of their new field. They now pride themselves in the use

BUT I CAN'T ARGUE THAT SIDE
OF THE CASE — IT'S NOT RIGHT.
I CAN'T TAKE THE SIDE OF
IMPRISONMENT AND TORTURE.

HMM— HERE'S JUSTIFICATION
FOR DETAINING THEM IN
REFUGEE CAMPS. THERE IS
NO "INTERNATIONAL RIGHT
OF ASYLUM." WE HAVE NO
LEGAL RESPONSIBILITY FOR
STATELESS PEOPLES.

LOCK 'EM UP
AND THROW AWAY
THE KEY!

of legal lingo, compete in trying to remember the names of esoteric cases mentioned in casebook footnotes and answer hypothetical questions by referring only to well-established legal precedent. Even when they get "res ipsa loquitur" mixed up with "proximate cause" the professor benignly encourages them. Now that they are all members of the same club he seems to feel that it matters little if it takes some longer to learn to knot their ties than others.

Final result:

The students have come full circle. Their sense of confusion and helplessness has given way to a swaggering feeling of power and exhilaration. They are back on top again, but this time they are thinking like lawyers.

Reason 13:
Intimate Pleasures—The Fall-Off Rate

*At a cocktail party during my second year I overheard
the following conversation between two young women:
  "What form of birth control do you use?"
  "Oh, I don't use any—my husband is a law student."*

Jeanne S. Stott
University of San Francisco School of Law
Currently: Small Claims Advisor

◆◆◆◆◆

Sexual Frequency If Married or Living with Someone:

Before Law School		*During Law School*
3 times per day	=	once a week
once a day		once a month
four times a week		New Year's Eve
once a week		don't hold your breath

Sexual Frequency If Single:

Before Law School		*During Law School*
once a day	=	once a semester
4 times a week (or less)		try masturbation

---

*If married to or living with another student, frequency rates should be halved.

Reason 14:

Stare Decisis, or You'll Wonder Where the Future Went When You Solve Each Case With Precedent

Law, horrible law, a miserable trial
Will make my next three years so hard to bear.

> Paul Cezanne
> Bourbon College, Faculty of Law (circa 1858)
> Became: Painter

Legal research is the most important skill learned in law school. This is because everything is solved, adjudicated or ordered in law from the bones of dead disputes. For example, while physicists, engineers and computer scientists deal with the exploration of space by stretching their minds forward to embrace the 21st century, lawyers retreat to their musty towers for the ghostest with the mostest.

To illustrate let's listen for a moment to a recent courtroom argument involving who was liable when a communications satellite got lost somewhere beyond Uranus:

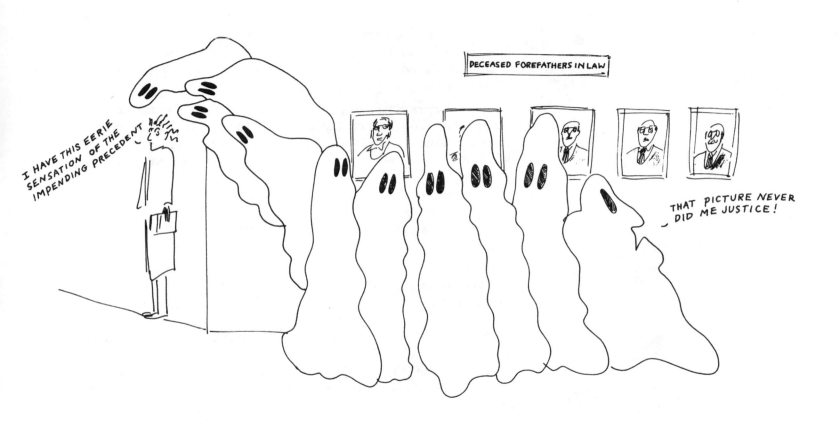

Lawyer 1 (representing the High Orbit Satellite Company): Your Honor, it's clear that what happened in this situation is on all fours with *Southern Arkansas Telephone v. Spotwood* decided in 1945. That learned decision involved a telephone pole which fell into the Tallapoosa River when a passing steamer snagged it on the . . .

Lawyer 2 (representing Straight Arrow Guidance, Inc.): Excuse me for interrupting, Your Honor, but the precedent that clearly controls the instant situation is obviously *Pathfinder Bob v. The Pony Express.* You see, just as my company made a good guidance for the satellite, the Pony Express gave Bob an accurate map. And just as Bob failed to traverse the open space between Saint Joseph's, Missouri, and Salt Lake City because of an Indian raid, the satellite was subjected to interference in outer space by a tribe of wild meteors . . .

Lawyer 3 (representing NoRisk Insurance of Wowsaw): As far as NoRisk is concerned, Your Honor, both of the cases cited by my learned brothers at the bar are merely fallacious, latter day interpretations of the *H.M.S. Petticoat Case* decided at Chancery in London in 1682. You see, while that decision involved a ship, not a satellite, and the problem developed when the Captain got into the rum, not when the computer failed, the whole affair took place on water instead of in space and the communication in question was a letter, not the transmission of television images, the two decisions establish exactly the same . . .

Need we say more?

Reason 15:

The Bar Exam

It was the second day of the bar exam. On my way up the hill to the examination room that sunny morning I realized that I'd rather be writing children's stories.

Peter Jan Honigsberg
New York University School of Law
Currently: Writer of children's folk tales

Imagine spending three years:
- ★ memorizing the contents of 26 feet, 7 inches of books (approximately 911 lbs., for those readers who are heavy thinkers),
- ★ listening to 1,800 hours of lectures,
- ★ taking thirty examinations, and
- ★ spending $25,000 – $50,000,

only to be told that all your reading, all your listening, all your money, and all your success on the examinations qualify you for absolutely nothing except the right to take one more exam—the Bar Examination.

Imagine now being told that the Bar Exam tests not so much what you learned in the 1,800 lecture hours or the 26 feet, 7 inches of books, but on your ability to completely memorize the contents of another eight-inch thick outline.

Imagine next being told that in order to get this "magic" outline, you must pay an additional $800 and spend a couple of months at another school.

Imagine going to this new school with the knowledge that even if you read the magic outline 18 yours a day, evict your teddy bear and sleep with the bar outline clutched to your breast, your chances of flunking the examination are one in two.

Imagine sitting in the Bar Examination for three days, surrounded by grey-faced classmates trying desperately to make it into the top 50 percent.

Imagine how you will feel if you succeed.

Imagine how you will feel if you fail.

Imagine how you will feel if you do something else entirely with your life.

Imagine how you will feel if you succeed.

Imagine how you will feel if you fail.

Imagine how you will feel if you do something entirely different with your life.

THE PRACTICE OF LAW

70

Reason 16:
No One Loves a Lawyer, or
Societal Disregard Through the Ages

People know instinctively something which honest lawyers dare not contemplate. The fact is that the law simply does not work, not for the average person. The law may in some circumstances and under some conditions work for government bureaucracies and giant corporations, but the average guy knows he is never going to get anything out of it but grief.

This helps to explain why people see lawyers as professional buzzards who prey upon people's troubles. It also helps to explain why lawyers tend to be such a joyless lot who often have trouble keeping even their own self-respect.

Lawyers may often do well, but not often by doing good . . . even when they try.

> Charles E. Sherman
> Boalt Hall School of Law, University of California
> Currently: Book Maker

I, Lucius Titus, have written this my testament without any lawyer, following my own natural reason rather than excessive and miserable diligence.

> The Will of a Citizen of Rome

It's better to enter the mouth of a tiger than a court of law.

> Ancient Chinese Proberb

St. Yves is from Brittany
A lawyer but not a thief
Such a thing is beyond belief

> A popular rhyme about a 14th century lawyer
> who was made a saint because he represented the poor

The first thing we do, let's kill all the lawyers.

> Shakespeare, Henry VI. Part II, Act iv

They have no lawyers among them for they consider them as a sort of people whose profession it is to disguise matters.

> Sir Thomas More, Utopia (1516), Of Law & Magistrates

That one hundred and fifty lawyers should do business together ought not to be expected.

> Thomas Jefferson, from his Autobiography (on the U.S. Congress)

Always remember that when you go into an attorney's office door, you will have to pay for it, first or last.

> Anthony Trollope, The Last Chronicle of Barset

73

The law is an ass.

Charles Dickens

I think we may class the lawyers in the natural history of monsters.

John Keats

Four sheep, a hog and ten bushels of wheat settled an Iowa breach of promise suit where $25,000 damages were demanded. The lawyers got all but the hog, which died before they could drive it away.

Item appearing in the Cheyenne *Leader*, January 14, 1888

Lawyer: One skilled in circumvention of the law.

Litigation is a machine which you go into as a pig and come out as a sausage.

Ambrose Bierce

Lawyers earn a living by the sweat of browbeating others.

James Gibbons Haneker

Lawyers: persons who write a 10,000 word document and call it a brief.

Franz Kafka

May your life be full of lawyers.

Mexican curse

For a good time, hire a hooker,
For a lot of time, hire my attorney.

Anonymous Prison Cell Graffiti

For a while you worried that a rich man with a cunning lawyer could no longer get ahead in this country.

But the Great American Dream is not moribund. Anyone who labors industriously and thinks deviously can go anyplace he chooses . . . That's why we have the Bill of Rights. Also the American Bar Association.

Art Spander
San Francisco Examiner, May 12, 1982

Reason 17:

Three Years is a Long Time to Train for Unemployment

I remember one job interview. The employer informed me that out of "hundreds" of applicants, they were interviewing fifty-four people for two positions. And because I was one of the lucky ones I had the opportunity to take a test— write three pages on whether there is an implied covenant to develop in a lease for land that turns out to have a yet unexplored geological formation. Huh? But I did it! I spent one entire day researching and writing on this question for a job with low pay, long hours, no creative outlet, minimal health coverage and only six vacation days per year. Amazingly, I got the job. Fortunately I had the common sense to turn it down.

Katherine M. Galvin
Boston College Law School
Currently: Director of a Committee Against U.S.
Intervention in Central America

Fighting for Clients

There can be few jobs since the internal combustion engine displaced a generation of blacksmiths that so many people have left so fast as the practice of law within the past decade. Of course, lots of lawyers have moved on to other endeavors not because they couldn't make a living before the Bar but because they found the legal profession to be unsatisfying, boring, or just too compromised by blatant schemes designed to separate average folks from their bank accounts. But beyond doubt, many more thousands of lawyers (many of them young) have taken other employment, not as a result of a sudden attack of altruism, but because there are too many lawyers and too few jobs. Indeed, so many people have hung law degrees on so many walls in the last few years that society is beginning to view lawyers as latter day locusts in three piece suits, multiplying even as they bound across the land with jaws flapping, writs at the ready and wallets extended.

Here are a few specifics:

★ There are 650,000 lawyers in the U.S.—one lawyer for every 383 people, including those in incubators, and nursing homes.

★ As you read this, there are 130,000 more embryonic lawyers in law school. (There were only 63,000 in 1968.)

★ Two-thirds of the lawyers in the world practice in the U.S.

★ The U.S. Department of Labor has estimated that by 1986, one of seven lawyers will be out of work.

★ By 1995, the U.S. will have over one million lawyers.

★ One of every three U.S. lawyers has been in practice less than **five** years.

* The cost of legal services accounts for 2 percent of the American gross national product—that's more than the output of the steel industry.
* Per capita, the U.S. has more than 3 times the lawyers than Great Britain (apparently the folks who invented so much of our legal mumbo-jumbo don't believe it to the extent we do) and 25 times more than Japan, which tells you more than you want to know about why their economy works and ours doesn't.
* There are more judges in Los Angeles County, California than in France.
* On a working day in the average large American city, one out of every one hundred human beings of all ages, races, sexes and sizes is a lawyer.
* Nine out of ten medical school graduates enter medical practice. But only five out of ten law school graduates go into law practice.
* *In the "more things change, the more they remain the same" category, we feel obliged to include the following from the Cheyenne, Wyoming, Leader of July 23, 1885:*

    "There are 11,000 lawyers in the state of New York.
    What an appalling state to be in."

SOON THEY'LL OUTNUMBER EVEN US!

Reason 18:

The Thesaurus—A Lawyer's Best Friend

A law dictionary defines legal terms.
A lawyer obscures them.
There is no difference.

Steve Mandel
University of Southern California School of Law
Currently: Book Distributor

Imagine that tomorrow you witness a nasty car accident and then describe it in a letter to a friend. Your letter might look like this:

Dear Max,

On my way to the theater yesterday, I saw this woman get creamed. A large truck ran a red light and hit her straight on. I was sure she was a goner, but even though she was thrown ten feet and probably broke an arm, she wasn't critically hurt. I stayed with her while the guy who ran the shop on the corner called . . .

Now, imagine that you witness the same accident four years from now, *after* you have passed the Bar and are an associate at Grumpy, Sleepy and Snoozy.

Dear Max,

    I witnessed some flagrantly tortious conduct today in which a female victim was smashed, battered, banged, beaten, pounded, punished, pummelled, pulped, pulverized, impaled, impacted, irritated, cut, cauterized, hit, hurt, mutilated, damaged, thumped and torn limb from limb when the driver of a huge, gargantuan, over-sized behemoth of an 18-wheeled vehicle, which can be described as either scarlet, cherry, vermillion, crimson, ruby, or blood-colored, negligently, dangerously, aggressively, illegally, irresponsibly, deliberately, unconscionably and carelessly drove, operated and inflicted said vehicle upon the victim with malice afore-thought, premeditation, conscious disregard of civilized amenities and just plain cussedness . . .

Bedtime prayers before Mommy went to law school.

AT THE PRESENT JUNCTURE, THIS DAY AND AGE, THIS HOUR, ON THIS, THE PRESENT OCCASION; I, MYSELF, THIS PARTICULAR INDIVIDUAL AND ENTITY, ALLEDGED TO BE MARY JOYCE HARCOURT AND SOMETIMES REFERRED TO AS "JOYCIE" OR "MOMMY" (MOTHER TO THE ALLEDGED LIBERTY REESE HARCOURT); REPOSIT, ASSIGN AND CONSIGN, FIX AND ESTABLISH THIS SAID PERSON, THE ABOVE AND AFORE-MENTIONED (SEE PARAGRAPH 1. LINE 3. WORDS 26, 27, 28) WHO SHALL BE REFERRED TO AS THE PARTY OF THE FIRST PART FROM THIS TIME FORWARD, IN A LOWERED (AS COMPARED TO UPRIGHT) RECLINED AND/OR PROSTRATED POSITION, FOR THE SOLE PURPOSE OF SLUMBER, REPOSE REST IN THE ARMS OF MORPHEUS, SOUNDLY AND/OR HEAVILY, LIKENED TO A TOP AND/OR LOG, NOT TO THE EXCLUSION OF DREAMING AND/OR SNORING WHICH SHALL REMAIN TO BE SEEN ON THE EVIDENCE OF THOSE WHO SHALL REMAIN ANONYMOUS AT THIS TIME; I, MYSELF, THIS PERSON, THIS PARTICULAR INDIVIDUAL AFOREMENTIONED AND NOW REFERRED TO AS THE PARTY OF THE FIRST PART, PROPOSE, REQUEST AND PETITION, MAKE BOLD TO ASK, PUT TO AND CALL UPON, COURT, SEEK TO ENTREAT, AND IMPLORE, BESIEGE, IMPORTUNE AND ADJURE, BEG AND BESEECH THE DIVINE DEITY, GODSHIP, GODHEAD, OMNIPOTENT AND OMNISCIENT SPIRIT i.e. SUPREME BEING, SOUL, HIGHER POWER, PROVIDENCE, KING OF KINGS, QUEEN OF QUEENS, LORD OF LORDS, ALMIGHTY ONE, ABSOLUTE BEING, INFINITE CAUSE, SOURCE, UNIVERSAL MIND, NATURE, ALL POWERFUL, ETERNAL BEING, ALL KNOWING, ALL WISE, ALL MERCIFUL, ALL HOLY, THE PRESERVER, MAKER, CREATOR, AUTHOR AND/OR CREATOR OF ALL THINGS, TRUTH AND LOVE; MY, THE AFOREMENTIONED PARTY OF THE FIRST PART, ESSENCE, FUNDAMENTAL TRUE BEING, INMOST NATURE, CORE, INNER AND ESOTERIC REALITY, VITAL CENTER, ESSENTIAL QUALITY AND SUCHNESS, QUIDDITY PITH, KERNEL, NUCLEUS, INMOST RECESSES OF THE HEART, SPIRIT, PRANA, LIFE FORCE; TO TAKE CUSTODY OF GUARD, WATCH OVER, SUSTAIN AND PRESERVE FOR THE SAFE KEEPING OF, AUSPICIOUS AND SECURE AND CAUTIOUS SURVEILLANCE OF, TO PROTECT, HOLD AND KEEP. SHOULD CIRCUMSTANCES WARRANT THAT I, THE AFOREMENTIONED ONE, NOW KNOWN AS THE PARTY OF THE PART, SHOULD EXPIRE, END, CEASE TO LIVE, EXTINGUISH THE MORTAL LIGHT, LEAVE THIS PHYSICAL PLANE, EXPERIENCE MY DEMISE, DESIST, QUIT THIS WORLD, MAKE MY EXIT, PASS ON, PASS AWAY, MEET MY END, SHUFFLE OFF THIS MORTAL COIL, RELINQUISH OR SURRENDER MY LIFE, YIELD THE GHOST, GIVE UP MY BREATH, GO OUT LIKE THE SNUFF OF A CANDLE, BEFORE OR AT A TIME PRIOR TO THE TIME I REGAIN CONSCIOUSNESS, PASS FROM THE SLEEPING TO THE WAKING STATE, ROUSE MYSELF, WARM TO THE DAY, OPEN MY EYES, I, THE PARTY OF THE FIRST PART, IMPLORE, BEG, AND BESEECH, INVOKE AND ENTREAT, HUMBLY ASK THEE ALMIGHTY, EVER PRESENT UNIFYER OF ALL PERSONS, PLACES AND THINGS, MAMMALS, FISH, BIRDS AND INSECTS, GIVER OF BOONS, INSTILLER OF FAITH, HEALING SOURCE, ONE WHO GIVES ENDLESS LOVE UNCONDITIONALLY, MY, AS IN ME AND MINE, AS IN I, THE PARTY OF THE FIRST PART, OF LOWER OR MORTAL NATURE, SPIRIT, ATMA, BUDDHI, VITAL FORCE, INNER PRINCIPLE, HEART, MIND AND EMBODIED BREATH, ANIMATING PRINCIPLE AND TRUE SELF, ESSENCE AND SUBSTANCE OF LIFE, THE DIVINITY THAT STIRS WITHIN, INNER FLAME AND SEAT OF CONSCIOUSNESS TO; (IF IT PLEASES THEE) APPROPRIATE, CAPTURE, SEIZE, ABDUCT WITH AND ACQUIRE FOR, AN INFINITE PERIOD OF TIME, ENTER INTO POSSESSION OF, AND TAKE RESPONSIBILITY FOR, OBTAIN AND RESCUE, PICK UP, GLEAN, GATHER IN, CAPTURE AND SEIZE AND HOLD UNTIL SUCH TIME AS IT SHALL BE RELINQUISHED BY THE SAID HOLDER. AMEN.

Bedtime prayers after Mommy went to law school.

Reason 19:
Beware the Law Siren's Song

*I dreamed that as a lawyer I would be a sort of warrior/
artist who fought for clients, but fought for justice above all.
Instead I found myself in a sort of ethical cave where
attorneys function as shadowy clerks spending their time
copying documents requested by their clients with little
regard to concepts of fairness and right. And perhaps even
more sadly, I discovered that the attorneys themselves were
all fungible, as interchangeable as their copying machines.*

F. Hayden Curry
University of Virginia School of Law
Currently: Artist/Builder

WARNING! Tie yourself to the mast, stuff your ears with bubble gum, cover your eyes with rounds of bologna. There is a seductress loose in the land who tempts the idealistic and attracts those who seek after truth and justice. Her song is simple—wrongs can be righted, causes can be launched and a new, more beautiful world forged by idealistic lawyers. Reality, unfortunately, is quite different. Law has tarried so long in the pockets of the "Powers That Be" that it has become the essential ingredient in the glue that binds us to the status quo. It makes a poor tool with which to effect change.

WARNING! Viewed from a distance, the Law Siren shimmers with many bright guises—all implying that anything is possible through the study and application of the law. The Siren is an expert at mirroring your own desire and will tell you exactly what you want to hear— that law can be used to create a new environmental order, to end all war, to desegregate schools, to protect the rights of the indigent, or whatever else is important to you. Viewed up close, this is patently not the case, but if you are close enough to the Law Siren to discover this, it will already be too late. You will be a lawyer.

WARNING! The Law Siren is dangerous precisely because she tells you that through the law you can fight for your beliefs in a way that will fulfill your most idealistic view of yourself, but still give you enough spare change to buy designer sunglasses. The hard truth is— the hungry need food, the homeless need shelter, and all the world needs peace, but no one needs more lawyers. If the 600,000 or so

lawyers already minted are not up to solving our problems, it's unlikely that you will help much. But what, you ask, about all the good and noble legal victories won by the Clarence Darrows of our legal tradition? You'd better get bigger pieces of Double Bubble for your ears—some of the Law Siren's music is obviously getting through.

To counter it let's look at a few areas where lawyers have honestly and zealously dedicated themselves to reforming the world by court order:

★ **Education:** *Brown v. Board of Education* ordered the desegregation of schools in 1954. Today the schools are more segregated than ever. If racial balance improves in the future it will be because people have learned to live with one another, not because a judge ordered it.

★ **Environment:** Major environmental lawsuits have been with us for at least two decades. Despite a few isolated victories, the forces that would abuse the air, water and land have hardly been slowed by a wave of the judicial wand. Again, we may clean up our act eventually, but not because we are told to by environmental lawyers.

★ **Poverty:** The first generation of bright, committed, hardworking legal aid lawyers became disillusioned and quit when they realized that every time they won a court victory guaranteeing one group of low income people more money, the government simply cut back another equally deserving program.

87

★ **Criminal Procedure:** *Gideon v. Wainwright* established that a low income person charged with any crime has the right to a lawyer. The result has been many thousands more public defenders, district attorneys and judges living off the public purse at great cost to the taxpayer. Just about the same percentage of low income defendants end up in jail as before they all had legal assistance.

Reason 20:

The Lawyer's First Commandment:
Keep Those Fees Up!

One of the partners circulated an advertisement for a book published by Prentice-Hall on how to make more money practicing law. It said:

"To the attorney who wants something more than the $50,000 a year most attorneys call success... Stop wasting time on unprofitable cases... It takes courage to drop clients, even though they're not as profitable as they should be. But you're not going to build your practice or make your fortune without courage."

Recognizing my cowardly nature, I resigned.

Anonymous
Harvard Law School
Currently: Librarian

The Scene:

A state senate hearing to consider proposed legislation to make it easier for non-lawyers to represent themselves in divorce proceedings. Although the public hearing was announced a month in advance, the time and place have been changed six times. The hearing finally convenes in an unmarked storage area in the Capitol basement.

Those Present:

Twelve members of the State Senate Judiciary Committee (all lawyers);

Six legislative assistants (four lawyers, two recent law school graduates studying for the Bar Exam at night);

Four representatives of various state agencies, including the Judicial Council, Administrator of the State Courts, the Attorney General's office and Office of Professional Standards (all lawyers);

Five representatives of interested private groups who wish to present testimony and were told of the room change, including the State Bar Association, the United Trial Lawyers, the Domestic Litigation Committee, the Association of Court Conciliators, and the Trial Judges Committee (all lawyers);

Three committee secretaries (two in night law school, one married to a lawyer); and

One member of the public, Abner Cristo, a janitor in state employ mopping behind a pile of discarded furniture in the corner (Abner is not a lawyer, though he once took a law school correspondence course

THE ALL NEW LAW REVIEW
I WANT MONEY
THAT'S WHAT I WANT
M-O-N-E-Y
LET ME EXPLAIN THE INHERENT DANGERS OF "DOING YOUR OWN DIVORCE".
BUT...
OBJECTION OVERRULED!
DON'T MOVE—
THIS COULD BE
YOUR BIG BREAK.

for six months. Unfortunately, he lost the matchbook containing the school's address and couldn't continue. Nevertheless, he regularly says "pursuant" and "moreover" and brings his two sandwiches and small bottle of muscatel to work in a gold-initialled briefcase).

Those Absent:

Representatives of several consumer organizations and Nolo Press, publisher of self-help law books, who as a result of an accidental oversight, were not notified of the room change and are all lost at various locations in the Capitol (one lawyer, two dropped-out lawyers and one earnest paralegal).

Opening Remarks
by the Chairperson of the Judiciary Committee:

"It has been brought to our attention that if we enact Senate Bill 312, the divorce law of this state can be easily simplified so that any fool who can get a drivers license can do his or her own without the need of a lawyer."

After two hours of testimony:

Closing Remarks
by the Chairperson of the Judiciary Committee:

"It seems absolutely clear to me, after listening to the enlightened testimony of the members of the general public, that there is no public sentiment in favor of simplifying divorce procedures, and that so doing might even cause economic hardship and unemployment to a certain deserving group of citizens. Let's table the divorce reform bill for this year, recess for lunch and then consider the Bar Association's proposal that all civil trials be conducted in Latin."

Reason 21:
Clients

You ask why I quit the practice of law?
  I hate conflict. Besides, what do I care about some
stranger, let alone his problems?

Denis Clifford
Columbia Law School
Currently: Author/Soldier of Fortune

Imagine that you have successfully graduated from law school. Those fellow students—the drudges, compulsive talkers, paranoids and dishonest competitors are now your professional colleagues at the Bar. However, the good company doesn't stop there. Now come the CLIENTS.

Clients come in assorted shapes and sizes—large, small, civil, criminal, plaintiff, defendant, incarcerated, inebriated, lacerated and so on. The one thing they all have in common is—a problem.

Domestic Clients: Are normally involved in a divorce, child custody, alimony or palimony dispute. They tend to be hostile, depressed, guilty, bitter, worried, vengeful or all six.

Probate/Estate Clients: Have often just lost a loved one and are usually feeling bereft, depressed, guilty, bitter, worried, vengeful or all six. In addition, they have all heard what a rip-off the probate process is and will be prepared to blame you. Because in your heart you know you are charging excessively for minimal services you will feel guilty enough to accept the blame.

Personal Injury Clients (legitimate): Most of these are in physical pain as well as depressed, worried, bitter and vengeful. They are delighted that you will take their cases for no money down and a percentage of the recovery until you win and they realize that after their medical bills have been subtracted from their share you somehow wound up with more money than they did, at which point they usually decide, with some justification, that you are a schmuck.

Personal Injury Clients (phony): The good thing about these people is that they are not in physical pain, depressed, worried, bitter or vengeful—they are merely greedy. The bad thing about them is that they have manufactured a fraudulent whiplash, twisted back or phobia and of course you ought to toss them out of your office unceremoniously. Perhaps you will, but when faced with trying to make a living in a world where it often appears that there are more

lawyers than clients, you might be tempted to join the 33.3% of lawyers that recent studies have shown are willing to counsel clients on phony personal injury claims.*

Criminal Clients: These people have been charged with being: rapists, burglars, murderers, pickpockets, arsonists, batterers and various and assorted other misdemeanants and felons. Many are guilty and with good reason feel persecuted, depressed, scared, angry, sullen, vengeful or all six. If you lose their case, as you will at least 80% of the time, they will rather regularly transfer their generalized hostility to you. Before long, most criminal lawyers have several guns and an unlisted phone number and begin to feel persecuted, depressed, angry, etc.

Business Clients: As a rule, these people are happier and richer than most other client types. They are nice to their spouses, good to their children and give to the United Way. They reserve their hostility for their business competitors who they would dearly love to draw, quarter and assault with plastique if it wouldn't put their comfortable lifestyle at risk. Instead when angry they phone their agent provocateur in charge of dispensing hostility—their lawyer.

Kansas City Times, August 4, 1981 from the article "The Lawyers" by Ron Ostroff.

99

Reason 22:
The Dream Killers:
Someone's Got To Do It

*How times have changed since the republic was founded.
Tell a lawyer today that you've just worked out a scheme
that will establish justice, promote domestic tranquility and
ensure the general welfare, and he'll end up persuading
you that if you're lucky and carefully follow his advice,
you may end up not going to jail.*

Robert Keller
Columbia Law School
Currently: Real Estate Novelist

Somebody eventually has to tell children that Santa Claus doesn't exist. Somebody has to prick the bubble of an unrealistic commercial venture. Somebody has to query and attempt to quantify all sorts of dreams and undertakings. Without doubt, being the finder of flaws is a skill that our society needs to have done well. That said, the more pertinent question becomes: Are you ready and willing to assume a career that is professionally committed to pessimism?

Suppose, for example, you do become a lawyer and two friends of yours, Sara and James, stop by to help you celebrate hanging out your first shingle. With stars in their eyes and beatific expressions on their faces they tell you that they too have some wonderful news—they've decided to move in together. About two seconds after you propose a toast the "what if" corner of your lawyer's brain compels you to furrow your brow, stroke your chin, and casually mention the Lee Marvin palimony case.

When Sara asks how movie stars fighting over millions of dollars affects them, you explain that the Marvin decision has established a precedent that boils down to the fact that to be legally safe, unmarried couples should put their understandings in writing.

You helpfully suggest that they:

★ inventory their separate possessions;
★ draw up an anticipatory property settlement agreement for use if they ever separate which delineates clearly whether income is to be shared equally or held separately;

★ design a rental agreement to cover James living in Sara's house, or in the alternative an agreement allowing James to buy into the house over time;

★ if and when they have a child, write a paternity agreement;

★ et cetera, et cetera.

When Sara and James leave you are feeling pleased that you have been able to contribute a bit of common sense to their star-struck venture.

A few days later James calls to thank you. It seems that when he and Sara sat down to deal with the legal realities of living together, they decided that they weren't quite ready to make the commitment after all. He then reiterates how grateful both he and Sara are for all of your good, practical advice and says how they owe their decision all to you. Finally he promises that they will have you over for supper real soon.

They never do.

Before

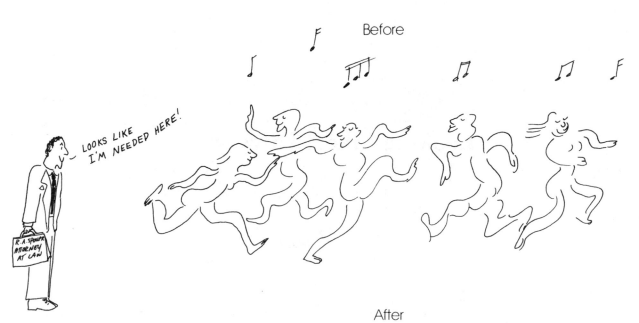

After

Reason 23:

Looking Like a Lawyer

*It was just so tedious dressing every morning as if I was
going to my own funeral.*

Anonymous
Valparaiso Law School
Currently: Between Careers

Question:
  Suppose you wanted 300 ordinary men and women—some vegetarian,
some black, some brown, some tall, some in wheelchairs, some
wearing T-shirts and sneakers, some riding motorcycles, some who
secretly want to be rock stars, artists or poets, to dress in blazers and
creased pants, wear glasses, speak briskly and unintelligibly in a strange
tongue, walk in a determined fashion in black shoes with square toes
and sensible heels (even on the golf course), carry one shoulder lower
than the other (the one attached to the arm carrying the hand-tooled
Italian briefcase), constantly check the digital watch on the other arm,
grind their teeth, interrupt whenever anyone begins to speak and carry
business cards on the ski slopes?

Answer:

Let them into law school, keep them three years, let them out.

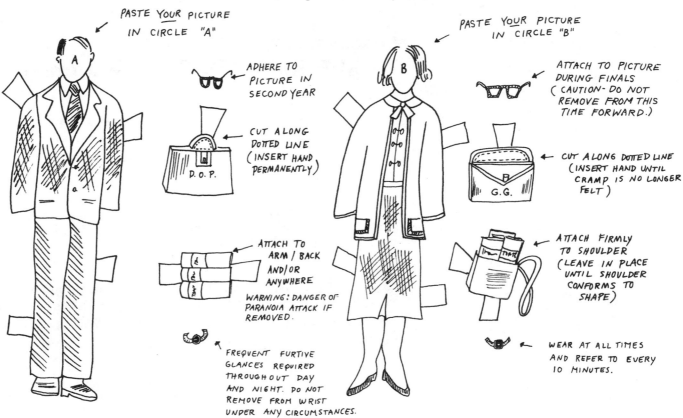

PASTE <u>YOUR</u> PICTURE
IN CIRCLE "A"

A

ADHERE TO
PICTURE IN
SECOND YEAR

CUT ALONG
DOTTED LINE
(INSERT HAND
PERMANENTLY)

D.O.P.

ATTACH TO
ARM/BACK
AND/OR
ANYWHERE

WARNING: DANGER OF
PARANOIA ATTACK IF
REMOVED.

FREQUENT FURTIVE
GLANCES REQUIRED
THROUGHOUT DAY
AND NIGHT. DO NOT
REMOVE FROM WRIST
UNDER ANY CIRCUMSTANCES.

PASTE YOUR PICTURE
IN CIRCLE "B"

B

ATTACH TO PICTURE
DURING FINALS
(CAUTION - DO NOT
REMOVE FROM THIS
TIME FORWARD.)

CUT ALONG DOTTED LINE
(INSERT HAND UNTIL
CRAMP IS NO LONGER
FELT)

G.G.

ATTACH FIRMLY
TO SHOULDER
(LEAVE IN PLACE
UNTIL SHOULDER
CONFORMS TO
SHAPE)

WEAR AT ALL TIMES
AND REFER TO EVERY
10 MINUTES.

Reason 24:
Legal Ethics—Up From Watergate

Legal ethics comes down to one word—money. Fairness, kindness, a commitment to helping people resolve their own disputes are all irrelevant. When I realized that even my best friend had an ethical duty to screw me if that's where the money was—I quit.

Barbara Moulton
George Washington University School of Law
Currently: Small Claims Advisor

When Richard Nixon, John Dean, John Erlichman, John Mitchell, Donald Segretti, Dwight Chapin and others were identified as participating in the events that became known as the Watergate scandal, many commentators noted that most were lawyers. More than one went on to suggest that this was no coincidence and that Watergate should be looked upon as confirmation of the fact that the average lawyer had ethics slightly below those of a pool hustler. Stung, the

organized bar decided to clean house. Never again would anyone be able to say that lawyers were unworthy of trust. One lawyer group which took particularly tough action was the American Judges Association—the professional group which represents American judges from the local courthouse to state supreme courts.

Bravely casting aside all suggestions that they choose a less qualified man, the judges elected Judge Dick C. P. Lantz as their President in November of 1981. As reported by the Washington Post, Mr. Lantz' qualifications included:

★ Frequent "unprovoked fits of temper," including berating and screaming at witnesses from the bench and ordering a lawyer to stay in court and proceed without a court reporter present when there should have been one.

★ Eating, drinking and talking on the telephone during a hearing.

★ Trying to get a friend into law school by appealing to a law professor who was in court before him.

★ Finding a lawyer in contempt of court for speaking Spanish to his client.

★ Ordering a $10,700 attorney's fee to be paid to his own election campaign manager, even though his friend withdrew as an attorney in the case.*

---

*All of these charges were made before the Florida Judicial Qualifications Commission. Lantz admitted several and pleaded no contest to the rest. Several attempts to block Lantz' elevation to the Presidency failed, but finally citing adverse press reports of his admitted misconduct, Lantz resigned on the day he was to take office.

Reason 25:

A Lawyer From the Client's Point of View

Rosemary, my client, was charged with D.U.I. If I was lucky, I could charge her six big ones. She was a stranger and I did my best to impress. I met her outside the courtroom in my deep blue Pierre Cardin. My act was together.

As we sat to chat, I noticed my ankles were bare. God, so did she! How stupid. I forgot my socks! (Not so stupid, really—in tropical Miami they make your feet feel clammy.) My act was blown.

"I don't want no sockless lawyer," she said as she shuffled off.

A guy could buy a lot of socks with $600, I thought disgustedly.

Glenn Terry
University of Florida College of Law
Currently: Cable Television producer and filmmaker

Let's tune in now as two business people discuss a dispute which happens to involve an improperly marked shipping container. The box which contained an alligator was mistakenly marked "delicious recipe" instead of "dangerous reptile." When a delivery boy thinking to score an index finger full of frosting lost a pinky instead, a lawsuit ensued.

The Freight Company Manager: When my legal beagle gets done chewing on your mouthpiece, he's gonna wish he'd left his dentures home in a glass.

The Animal Shipping Company Director: You got no chance. I hired Mean Joe Greenowski—he's so tricky, he not only speaks Greek, he reads minds. He can take one look at your shyster and know whether he's gonna claim contributing nonsense or mitigating circumcision.

FCM: Oh yeah, I got Hot Dog McGraw—he draws the fastest, nastiest writ in the West. He can pound the table, raise an objection, and chop up an opposing witness faster and louder than...

ASD: So, big deal, let's really get down to it. What does Hot Dog charge? Mean Joe just raised his fees to $500 an hour and you know that a man who has the balls to charge that much has got to be a winner.

FCM: Okay, you win. I'll settle. Hot Dog must be getting a little past it—he's only billing $425. Anybody as soft as that obviously can't cut the mustard.

Reason 26:
You Might End Up Marrying (or Living With) Another Lawyer

Ever since law school I've been accused of needing to have the last word. It's not that I'm an argumentative sort. I never articulate any position unless considering the totality of the circumstances it is irrefutable. The man I live with—a defense attorney wouldn't you know—often doesn't see the logic of my positions. Of course, he usually adopts his views based on prejudice, bias and emotion.

Irene Takahashi
King Hall School of Law, University of California
Currently: Federal Prosecutor (retired)

Imagine what it would be like to become a lawyer and then marry one. It could happen to you as lawyers often pair off. There are two reasons for this: (1) other lawyers don't ask for free legal advice, and (2) non-lawyers generally avoid lawyers on social occasions because they are contentious, boring, and never offer to pay.

Come with us now as we join newlyweds Barry (University of Tennessee School of Law '78) and Laverne (Cornell University School of Law '81) as they attempt to put aside their professional personas to enjoy a tranquil breakfast.

Barry: This is rather tasty french toast, dear, but didn't we agree to have raisin toast on weekends instead of wheat?

Laverne: Oh, honey, I think you're remembering our agreement a little wrong. What we really decided was to have raisin toast on the weekend mornings that we didn't have french toast—everyone knows you can't make french toast with raisin bread, silly!

Barry: I don't see why not and anyway we unequivocally agreed on weekends with raisin toast—I've been relying on it all week! Indeed I might even say that I've suffered genuine and irreparable pain and...

Laverne: No need to get adversarial, my dear. Now I'm sure we can work out a sensible compromise.

Barry: Well, how about having raisin toast every Sunday morning except that on the mornings we have french toast you can pick the raisins out of your pieces?

Laverne: You call that a compromise? I suggest...

Reason 27:

Becoming a Partner

My enjoyment of practicing law with a good-sized firm was hampered by three factors: I didn't like the work, I didn't like the other lawyers, and I didn't like the clients. Nothing I've done in the years since I quit the law has been nearly as boring.

Robert Flaherty
University of Michigan Law School
Currently: Restaurateur

Everyone who has ever read a book by Louis Auchincloss knows about the rewards of getting to be a partner in a big firm—the $200,000 draw (in a bad year), membership in the yacht club, March in Miami, et cetera. Unfortunately, while being a senior partner isn't too hard to take (except for your colleagues), getting to be one is not easily accomplished. Here are some helpful hints:

Hint 1: Start Early. Plan to be born white, male and Protestant. If you can't manage this try female, black, buddhist and handicapped—it's hard for even the stuffiest old line firm to resist a quadruple minority if, in addition, she is also the editor of the Harvard Law Review (see Hint 2, below).

Hint 2: Character is Formed in Kindergarten. Not only must you pile your blocks higher than any of the other kids, you must also learn to kick over the piles of the other smart kids without getting caught. Later this will be called "aggressive advocacy." Your only goal in your school years is to be number one in everything so that you are sure to be accepted at Yale (Harvard, Princeton and about thirteen other schools will also work, but if you have to ask which ones, consider setting your sights on the legal department of a good-sized insurance company in the Midwest).

Hint 3: The Rewards of Abstinence. When you reach Yale, you must study maniacally so that you graduate with honors, get 750 on your law boards, and are accepted at Harvard Law School (there are six, maybe seven other law schools that will keep you on the partnership ladder and a thousand or so others that won't).

Hint 4: Law Review is a Must. Not only must you study 20 hours a day, so as to place in the top 10 percent of all your desperately over-achieving classmates and be selected for the law review, your law review contribution must demonstrate that you are politically sound (it helps to say a kind word about feudalism, or, if you want to be daringly modern, William Howard Taft).

Hint 5: What to Wear at Your Employment Interview. This is critical. More than one law review editor has blown it all by wearing a blue shirt to this interview. Men should be sure to wear ties covered with small pheasants (mallards in flight are acceptable, but crossed golf clubs almost guarantee that you will end up working for a small firm in the suburbs). Women should absolutely avoid Gucci, Pucci, or even Yves Saint Laurent and instead wear sensible tweeds in the style favored by the English royal family in 1938.

You are doing great so far. You should now be an associate at the firm of Adams, Adams & Fudge. But don't relax—the ladder still stretches far above you and each ascending rung is more slippery than the one below. You must realize that most associates don't make it all the way to full partner but are let go when their youthful fire and energy begin to ebb. Why? Mostly because they are just not tough enough. But back to specifics.

Hint 6: Energy is as Important as Intelligence. Always stay at work until nine in the evening and be sure to show up first on Saturday mornings. In the more liberal big firms, it is permissible to wear a blue shirt on the weekends.

Hint 7: Making the Most of the Old School Tie. If you went to Princeton, Amherst or Stanford (West Coast only), have your alumni magazine delivered to your office. If you went to college at Cornell or UCLA, it's best to have it sent to your home.

Hint 8: Never Be Seen in the Wrong Court. If you play racquet-ball, quickly change to squash without telling anyone. If you play tennis, be sure you use a wood racquet. If you play polo, a small picture of your horse should be placed in a modest silver frame on the corner of your desk.

Hint 9: Learn to Order Lunch in Italian. Of course, we assume that you already know French. If you don't, you will probably want to resign quietly, although you may be able to get by for a while by announcing that as long as the Frogs vote socialist, you will never eat another bite of cassoulet (kass-oo-lay).

Hint 10: Save Your Money. You will be paid as much as $40,000 from the start and will get generous raises. Unfortunately, it probably won't last. Big firms are never so crude as to fire anyone, of course. But when your cubicle is reduced to a broom closet, it occurs to you that your secretary, who mysteriously disappeared two years ago, will never be replaced, and you haven't had Oysters Rockefeller and Pommes Frites with a partner since you had that trouble with the Collingworth bonds, you will reluctantly realize that at 35 you have a lot of knowledge about municipal financing, a bad stomach, high child support payments, an over-developed taste for Wild Turkey, tendonitis (from all that squash), and that almost without noticing it you have been transformed from an "up and coming" to a "down and going." Unfortunately, you have little experience and few legal skills which are valuable outside the world of Big Firms, and therefore are probably unemployable as a lawyer. (No big firm will ever hire anyone eased out by another, of course.) Your best bet is probably to apply for a teaching job at a law school—this being the only place that could possibly be interested in a specialty as narrow as yours.

Reason 28:
How It Is Ten Years After Law School

I quit law after practicing for eleven years. My conclusion: If you want to find the law, go to law school. If you want to find justice, go to Small Claims Court.

Paul Rosenthal
Hastings College of Law
Currently: Owner/Chef, The Crossroads Restaurant

Harry: Hi, Elaine, I don't think I've seen you since the Bar. How have you been doing?

Elaine: Great, terrific, or at least since my second divorce. You know I'm with Grin & Barrett now. We're a pretty hot ticket in corporate debentures. Of course, I put in my twelve hours, but then, you've got to if you really want to make partner, and I do. My life isn't all work of course. I stay busy by jogging, pumping the nautilis machines, A.A., EST, Professional Singles, Women Organized to Protest Racism, Sexism, & Coffee, as well, of course, as Bar Association Meetings, Continuing Education of the Bar lectures and Trancendental Meditation.

fig. 1 (NORMAL BRAIN)

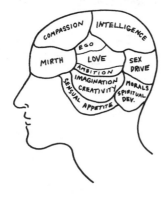

Before

fig. 2 (LAWBOTOMIZED BRAIN)

After

But what are you doing, Harry?

Harry: Oh, since I quit law and became a waiter, I have a lot of time to myself.

Elaine: You really quit being a lawyer to become a waiter?

Harry: Sometimes I feel a little badly about my loss of status, but then, making $40,000 a year, most of it tax-free, for a 25-hour-a-week job is some compensation. Of course, sometimes I do miss jogging.

Elaine: You quit jogging?

Harry: What could I do? They only let lawyers, doctors, accountants and coke dealers in the marathons these days. Apparently they found that they're the only people compulsive enough to have a chance.

Reason 29:
You Might Get to Be a Judge

Aside from the biblical warning that it is almost sure to come back to haunt you, there are several more practical reasons why donning the robe is a downer:

★ *you will have to listen to all those attorneys you used to avoid at cocktail parties;*

★ *the robes itch;*

★ *none of your friends will share a joint with you; and*

★ *you will be moved to an almost uncontrollable urge to violence every time someone says "here come de judge."*

Doug Hill
Boalt Hall School of Law, University of California
Currently: Publisher, *Berkeley Monthly*

Let us share with you a page from the forthcoming new book, *Pontificating From Above—A Student's Guide to Jobs in the Field of Shouting Down at People from Platforms.* We will skip the sections on ministers, circus barkers, tennis referees and college lecturers and turn directly to judges. It reads:

> While it's true that law school is a bore, studying for the Bar Exam miserable, and practicing law unbelievably petty and full of tacky little details, it will all be worthwhile if you have the foresight to make friends with the right politician and are appointed to the bench. Now this is a platform worth aspiring to. Among the principal advantages of the job are:
>
> You get to spend up to eight hours a day looking out at the world from a really splendid, elevated throne.*
>
> You get to dress in a handsome black nightgown, appropriately funereal, which scares many of the people who come to talk to you. See our English edition for information about those lovely white wigs that have sadly been eliminated in the colonies.

---

*In the spirit of accurate reporting, however, it must be conceded that the throne isn't quite what it used to be before the Media robbed the world of its love and respect for elevated authority. Indeed, there are some who have the bad taste to point out that it's little more than a pine box at the end of a drafty municipal hall. There is obviously no need to respond in detail to this sort of killjoy.

A Day in the Fantasy Life of a Judge

You get your own dandy little hammer which you are free to bang briskly whenever anyone is the least bit impolite.

Your former law school classmates, even the haughtiest ones, must stand when you climb onto your throne. Even better, they must call you "Your Honor" and if they are really anxious that you do something, say "Pray the Court" or "May it please the Court." Unfortunately, kneeling and bowing have been eliminated.

Best of all, if anyone speaks to you roughly or is disrespectful of your authority, you get to exorcise your accumulated frustrations by nodding down to your armed bailiff (a comfortably big former junior college football player who does his best to keep the local brewery solvent) and he will grab the impolite fellow and put him in a steel cage. This almost always has a salutary effect on the other people who come before you who are now much more willing to conduct themselves in a properly obsequious manner.

You Will Learn To Be a Creative Accountant

I spent a fascinating four years as a small cog in a large law machine where the income each young associate (often called a "profit center") produced was supposed to exceed their cost to the firm by a substantial amount. This was necessary to com-pensate for those senior partners for which the reverse was true.

Doug Carlston
Harvard Law School
President, Broderbund Software

*****

If you enter practice with a private firm, you will quickly be taught how to keep two sets of books: one for your clients, the other for your boss. The idea, of course, is that the firm will want to bill your clients for a highly exaggerated number of hours, while paying you for as few as possible. Read on and you will get some insight into why the Mafia calls lawyers "the Mob."

UNIT BILLING: This billing system requires a unique lawyer's clock which contains no division smaller than the quarter hour (truly advanced firms only use half-hour clocks). It works like this: No matter what portion of a quarter hour is spent on a particular client's business, you will compute your billing time to the next quarter hour. Thus, if you talk to a client for three minutes on the phone, you bill for 15 minutes. If the call lasts 16 minutes, you bill for a half-hour, and so on.

BILLING LAWYER RATES FOR SECRETARY TIME: Most legal jobs involve a hefty amount of repetitive paper shuffling and form preparation which can be accomplished by a bright chimpanzee. Your firm, which will grudgingly pay you $40,000 per year ($20 per hour) while it bills your clients $150 per hour for your time, will expect you to unload as much work as possible on your secretary or paralegal, who gets paid $10 per hour.

EFFICIENCY BILLING: This is the current rage at large law firms. Efficiency billing works like this. You compute how long it takes you to accomplish a legal task the first time you do it. Say you tackle a Clifford trust and the initial one takes three hours. Fair enough! Ten trusts later, you will probably be able to accomplish the same task in 17 minutes. Terrific, but don't forget to bill your client for the entire three hours. This is thought to be extremely efficient for the firm.

Bonus Reason:

The Law Pound

When you first suggested I compare law students and certain types of dogs, I came up with several ideas. Then it struck me. Considering some of the products of law school I've known over the years, the whole concept seemed to be a monumental insult to the canine race. I refuse to participate further.

Steve Elias
Hastings College of Law,
University of California
Currently: Lexicographer

ANYONE FOR A DEBATE?

CRUNCH!

Surely you have noticed how much some people resemble domestic animals. On the theory that it's possible to tell a lot about a person's character by paying attention to this sort of similarity, let's visit a first-year law school class and see what sorts of dogs we meet.

DOBERMAN DOUG: Contrary to popular belief, the sort of aggressive personality that attacks everything that moves is not dominant in law school. Nevertheless, our adversary legal system, like pro football and the private armies of certain religious leaders, attracts a number of people who don't seem to feel alive unless they see blood on the floor. You should be able to recognize this type easily.

BLOODHOUND BILL   BULLDOG BETH   SCHNAUZER SALLY

After eagerly dissecting points made by others in class discussion, they can't suppress a big toothed smile.

BLOODHOUND BILL: There is nothing smart about a bloodhound. It succeeds precisely because it's too dumb to quit sniffing myopically after its quarry, no matter how much time has elapsed or how much discomfort it has encountered. This sort of law student always arrives at school early, leaves late, underlines every second word in their texts with a yellow magic marker and finishes towards the bottom of the class. However, once they pass the bar exam on the third try, they really blossom. In a profession where to be both sensitive and intelligent is usually to drop out, they do exceedingly well.

BULLDOG BETH: Do you know people with true one-track minds? No matter what the conversation, they seize on a single point and return to it *ad nauseum.* All too often, their fixation involves something like the evils of fluoride in the water or coercive methods of potty training. Fortunately, there are only about 30 of this type in the entire law school. Unfortunately, if you decide to matriculate, one will inevitably be assigned to the seat next to you.

SCHNAUZER SALLY: In case you re a mite hazy on your dog breeds, a Schnauzer is a pesty little type A beast which never shuts up. When it's proud of itself, it goes "yip, yip, yip." When it's annoyed or wants something (usually unreasonable), it goes "yap, yap, yap." This type is both common and successful in law school. Their approach is often characterized as "winning through whining."

The Ten Best Lawyer Jokes

A woman diagnosed as having a brain tumor was told by her doctor that she would need the transplant of a one-pound brain. The doctor then asked, "What type of brain do you want?"

"What type?"

"Yes," replied the doctor. "There is a substantial difference in price. For example, a one-pound brain of a surgeon costs $60,000, while you can get a one-pound truck driver's brain for $20,000, and so on."

"Can you give me a one-pound lawyer's brain? Ever since I was a little girl, I've dreamed of being a trial attorney."

"That's $250,000," the doctor replied.

"Why so much?" the woman asked. "That's over four times what a surgeon's brain costs."

"Do you have any idea how many lawyers it takes to produce a pound of brain?" the doctor replied.

*****

Renfro took his poorly trained dog to the Pavlov Obedience School.

"Your dog can be trained to be anything you'd like him to be," said Pavlov.

"Please demonstrate," said Renfro.

Pavlov took a bunch of bones, threw them on the ground and called, "Here, Harry." An animal rushed out, seized the bones, and in no time built a bridge.

"That dog was trained for an engineer," announced the dog trainer.

"Amazing!" said Renfro.

Pavlov dismantled the bones, threw them on the ground, and called another dog. This animal constructed a skeleton.

"His owner is a doctor," said Pavlov.

"Unbelievable," responded Renfro.

Suddenly, a third dog rushed up, promptly ate all the bones and then screwed the other two dogs.

"Great scott!" exclaimed Renfro. "Who owns that dog?"

"Oh, that one is being trained for a divorce lawyer!" Pavlov responded.

*****

A man approached the Pearly Gates and was met not only by St. Peter, but by the entire heavenly host, with Jesus himself looking over a cloud.

"What did I do to deserve such a greeting?" the man asked.

"You're the oldest lawyer who has ever entered here," St. Peter replied.

"What do you mean, the oldest? Why, I died very young. I was only 43," the man said indignantly.

"Not according to the hours you billed," St. Peter responded.

*****

A doctor and a lawyer were talking at a party. Their conversation was constantly interrupted by people describing their ailments and asking the doctor for free medical advice. After an hour of this, the exasperated doctor turned to the lawyer.

"What do you do to stop people from asking you for legal advice when you're out of the office?"

"I give it to them, and then I send them a bill," replied the lawyer.

The doctor was shocked, but agreed to give it a try.

The next day, still feeling slightly guilty, the doctor prepared several bills. When he went to place them in his mailbox, he found a bill from the lawyer.

*****

In the men's room of an exclusive country club, two lawyers were in adjoining stalls, when one noticed that there was no toilet tissue.

"Hey, George," he called, "Hand me some paper, will you?"

A disturbed voice replied, "Gosh, there isn't any here, either."

"Any newspaper laying around?"

"No, I don't see any."

"Do you have an old envelope in your pocket? A letter maybe?"

"Sorry."

"Well then, do you have two fives for a ten?"

A lawyer named Strange was shopping for a tombstone. After he made his selection, the stonecutter asked him what inscription he would like on it.

"Here lies Strange, an honest man and a lawyer," responded the lawyer.

"Sorry, but I can't do that," replied the stonecutter. "In this state, it's against the law to bury two people in the same grave. However, I could put 'Here lies an honest lawyer.'"

"But that won't let people know who it is," protested the lawyer.

"Certainly will," retorted the stonecutter, "People will read it and exclaim, 'That's Strange!'"

*****

For three years, the young attorney had been taking his brief vacations at this country inn. The last time he'd finally managed an affair with the innkeeper's daughter. Looking forward to an exciting few days, he dragged his suitcase up the stairs of the inn, then stopped short. There sat his lover with an infant on her lap!

"Helen, why didn't you write when you learned you were pregnant?" he cried. "I would have rushed up here, we could have gotten married and the baby would have my name!"

"Well," she said, "when my folks found out about my condition, we sat up all night talkin' and talkin' and decided it would be better to have a bastard in the family than a lawyer."

*****

Question: How many lawyers does it take to change a lightbulb?
Answer: How many can you afford?

*****

An attorney with a leaky sink called his local plumber for repairs. After working on the sink for 15 minutes the plumber said: "All fixed; that'll be $100 bucks."

The lawyer replied: "My gosh! That's more money than I make an hour."

The plumber then retorted: "I know; that's why I quit being a lawyer."

*****

A storm raged along a rugged sea coast where a crowded passenger ship is smashed on a reef one hundred yards from shore. On the desk, the captain, a priest and a lawyer look across the shark-filled waters, trying to decide who will swim to shore with a line in order to haul the ship to safety.

The captain says, "I'll go first, I'm a man of the sea. I know the currents and creatures of the deep." He ties a line around his waist and jumps over the side. He hardly hits the water before an enormous great white shark opens its jaws and swallows him whole.

The priest steps forward and says, "I'm a man of god. I'll be protected." He dives into the water and sinks in a flurry of fins and foam.

Finally the lawyer fastens a line to his belt and leaps into the sea. The sharks part and he swims calmly to shore.

As he struggles into the beach, one of the rescuers cries, "It's a miracle!"

"Miracle, hell" replies the lawyer, "It's professional courtesy."

About the Authors:

Ralph Warner, Boalt Hall School of Law, University of California, is currently a writer and publisher.

Toni Ihara, King Hall School of Law, University of California, is currently a graphic designer and writer.

About the Artist:

Mari Stein, who never quite completed her law school application, is currently an artist, writer and yoga teacher.

About the Publisher:

Nolo Press is a pioneer self-help law publisher with offices in Berkeley and Occidental, California. It is dedicated to the idea that with competent information there is a great deal that people can do to solve their own legal problems. Nolo publishes about 30 self-help law books and the Nolo News, an eclectic legal newspaper. For a catalogue and a free Nolo News, write Nolo Press, 950 Parker Street, Berkeley, CA 94710, or Nolo Press, Box 544, Occidental, CA 95465.

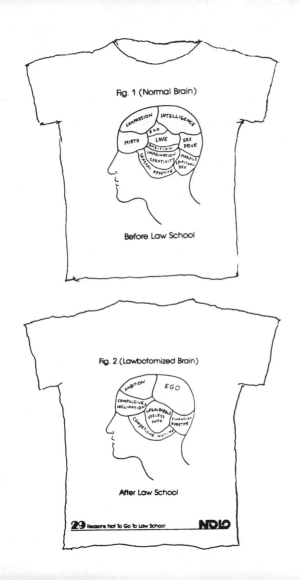

For Your Lawbotomy T-Shirt

Send $7.95 each _____

Tax (CA only; San Mateo, L.A., Santa Clara & Bart counties 6½%, others 6%) _____

Postage & Handling _____$1.00_____

TOTAL ━━━━━━━━

number of shirts _____; color: **black**
size ☐sm.   ☐med.   ☐lg.   ☐x-lg

Nolo also publishes a complete line of self-help law books.

☐ Please send me a free catalog

Send to: **Nolo Press**
            950 Parker Street
            Berkeley, CA 94710